MW00414049

MISSISSIPPI

The Microcosm of America

*Dedicated to Emmett Till
and all the children of Mississippi.*

*Special thanks to Barry Segal,
your support changed everything.*

MISSISSIPPI
The Microcosm of America

*We need all hands on deck to get
white supremacy off the necks of Black people."*

Rev. Dr. Jacqui Lewis

MISSISSIPPI

The Microcosm of America

PREFACE

Genesis Be's clarion call in "Mississippi: The Microcosm of America" has ignited people's hearts, minds, and passions around the United States.

I have traveled with her to dozens of states and witnessed, firsthand, the power of this message scores of times. The truth of the content and care by which Genesis delivers these words are perfectly matched.

In this poem, we are reminded that we are connected to one another. We are called to embrace the past with open eyes and the future with open hearts working toward inclusion, kindness, and empathy.

Doug Pagitt
Vote Common Good

MISSISSIPPI
The Microcosm of America

Copyright © 2021
Genesis Be | Common Good Coalition
All Rights Reserved

ISBN: 978-1-7371828-0-1

Genesis Be
genesisbe@gmail.com

Layout & Design
Tim Gilman | timmyroland.com

Strive Till I Rise
strivetillirise.org

Common Good Coalition
cgcoalition.com

MISSISSIPPI

The Microcosm of America

a poem by
Genesis Be

MISSISSIPPI

The Microcosm of America

Mississippi is a
microcosm of a nation

Police exoneration
and mass incarceration

Black and brown bodies

A commodity

Mothers separated
from babies

Border policies

MISSISSIPPI
The Microcosm of America

Quoting Bibles
& false prophecies

Our White House is
painted with the
Klan's ideology

Our leadership

Exploiting
white poverty

MISSISSIPPI

The Microcosm of America

Keeping us
separate and divided

Gay versus Straight

White versus Black

Based on fear and far
from the facts

MISSISSIPPI

The Microcosm of America

See, I hail from
a State

Called the
Mighty Mississippi

Our State flag
holds the stars

And bars

Praising a
brutal history

MISSISSIPPI
The Microcosm of America

It flies in front
of schools

And in my
judges court

Sending a clear
message to us

Our lives are not
important

MISSISSIPPI
The Microcosm of America

Cause my Dad
was only five

When the Klan
drived by

Bust bullets into
his house

With six children inside

On the back of
the truck

A Confederate flag
flyin high

These are the truths
you choose to deny

MISSISSIPPI
The Microcosm of America

See Mississippi,
like America

Eats your child
and mine

The white supremacist lie

Is a prison of your
own design

You forfeited your
humanity

In order to
deny mine!

MISSISSIPPI

The Microcosm of America

See Mississippi is a
Microcosm of a Nation

That Gaslights this
generation

Where I am from,
children walk across
stages

At their own
graduations

With a racist
symbol waivin

MISSISSIPPI

The Microcosm of America

Just the display
is sayin

We are forgotten
and forsaken

Disrespected
on the daily

Decades
of discrimination

With lynchings and
devastation!

MISSISSIPPI

The Microcosm of America

Your supremacy
is a lie

You accepted it

A confederate
curse

You inherited

MISSISSIPPI

The Microcosm of America

Bigotry is blinding

Your fear of
the other

Has blocked your
own blessings

From sisters
& brothers

MISSISSIPPI

The Microcosm of America

Outrage fatigue

I'm screaming
I can't breathe

From the top it
trickles down

To our judges
and police

MISSISSIPPI
The Microcosm of America

Cause the illusion
of freedom

Is far more dangerous

Than any jail cell or
cramped cages

Yes Mississippi is
a microcosm of
my Nation

MISSISSIPPI

The Microcosm of America

Where cowards
replace white sheets

With fake avatars

Repeating their
parent's folklore

Tooth fairy
santa clause

MISSISSIPPI

The Microcosm of America

Your history's white
washed

Google black codes
and by-laws

In the comment section
sound off

SOUND OFF!

MISSISSIPPI

The Microcosm of America

They call me a nipper
a bitch or a dyke

Call me whatever
you like

I been through worse
in this fight

The hatred in your words
just proves that
I'm right

MISSISSIPPI

The Microcosm of America

Mississippi is a microcosm
of a country

That always needed me
but never wanted me

My melanin and skin
is a sin

Sentenced to build
your economy

MISSISSIPPI

The Microcosm of America

Pack the prisons fill
the quotas

Make us felons

Never voters

Travel bans
and deportations

Killer cops no
resignation

No federal Indictment
just mock trials

MISSISSIPPI
The Microcosm of America

My heart bleeds as
the billboard reads

Make America
white again

As my favorite
rapper concedes

Making me question
everything that I believe

MISSISSIPPI
The Microcosm of America

And still,
I love America

Cause I have hope

Some choose to
jump ship

And some steer
the boat

MISSISSIPPI
The Microcosm of America

I know that love and
humanity lives

In the smile
of every child

In the heart
of every kid

Be brave enough to
break the curse

MISSISSIPPI

The Microcosm of America

We need you at
the polls

Out in droves

Voting against the
bigots you oppose

MISSISSIPPI
The Microcosm of America

Study law,
run for office

Use your voice,
write your Congress

Make a call,
choose a march

Malcolm's gone,
grab the torch

MISSISSIPPI
The Microcosm of America

Read a book,
write a rap

Speak with truth
and deal with facts

Freedom & justice
are under attack

MISSISSIPPI

The Microcosm of America

Alt right affiliation

Of Trump's
administration

Confederate
infiltration

Neo Nazis
showing faces

Fueling the fear
and hatred

While expanding their
corporations

MISSISSIPPI

The Microcosm of America

Do you see now . . .

how . . .

Mississippi
is a microcosm
of our Nation?

COMMONGOOD
COALITION

———

Common Good Coalition is a network of creative, motivated, and courageous professionals. We are artists, business people, and religious leaders who are committed to the common good. We can no longer wait to shift the conversation.

We gather and partner to share our stories, articulate our values, and bring a compassionate and healing perspective to today's complex issues. Our goal is to help others--and ourselves--to modify perceptions and perspectives and inspire change.

cgcoalition.com.

about Genesis Be

In 2016, a young rapper from Mississippi captivated America with a bold theatrical protest against the Mississippi State Flag. The protest went viral. The resulting backlash and press, threw her into the ongoing fight to remove the Confederate emblem from the Mississippi State Flag. Publications such as *The Associated Press, New York Times, NY Daily News, ABC News, VICE Impact* have featured her, sharing her message of racial healing, gender equality, and youth empowerment. She is the subject of *Mississippi Turning* (2022) a documentary produced by Breakout & Moral Courage Porject. *She* continues to **facilitate civil discourse** to improve race relations in her home state Mississippi.

In 2020, her collaborative effort saw a historical victory when Mississippi changed its State Flag after flying over 120 years.

Genesis Be has recently completed two college tours and two National tours wherein she explores the threats and media push back for her grassroots efforts to unite young Mississippians against White Supremacy. She is also giving audience members tools and exercises to help engage those with opposing views to manifest a solution based outcome, rather than just fighting online. Her intersectionality as a biracial queer woman of color from the deep south, allows her to explore and express concepts that audiences have deemed an extraordinarily "unique and compelling lense."

MISSISSIPPI

The Microcosm of America